MIDDLE CLASS ★ UNION MADE

Richard A. Levins

ISBN 0-9767054-4-3

MIDDLE CLASS ★ UNION MADE

INTRODUCTION

If the United States is to remain a successful economic model for the world, we will have to pay greater attention to restoring and sustaining the middle class. Government must help with this task, but it cannot do it alone. Strong and effective unions are an essential part of any strategy that will restore and maintain the American middle class.

In the Fall of 2005, I pulled into a filling station near my house in Minneapolis. In three months, gas had increased in price by 50 cents per gallon. Everything I saw on the news said the price I was paying that day would soon look like a bargain. During the hour or so I ran errands, combined profits of our ten largest energy companies ballooned another $13.5 million. Meanwhile, Congress had just served up another heaping portion of tax breaks to those same corporations.

Across the street from the station, the thrift

3

shop's large parking lot was filled with cars. Hundreds of people were taking advantage of a sale on used back-to-school clothing. Those of slightly better means flocked to the new Wal-Mart a few blocks away to buy whatever had come in on the most recent boat from China. The Wal-Mart makes its home where a more middle-class, but failed, shopping center stood just a year ago. Surrounding retailers wonder how much longer they can afford to pay union-scale wages now that their low-wage neighbor has opened for business.

I drove back to our house that originally sold new for around $10,000 and was well within the means of a blue-collar family with one wage earner. My wife and I purchased the house when it was over 45 years old and in need of substantial work, paying more than ten times the original price. Five years later, the house can be sold for twice what we paid. A blue-collar family with a single wage earner cannot dream of buying the house now without public assistance and all of the attendant risks. Through all this, the house has remained what it always has been—a place to live. The additional value is of no use whatsoever to us. Before the mortgage was paid off, the high value was a benefit mostly to the mortgage company because it meant higher payments to them. We, on the other hand, had less money to spend on other things during the years we made payments on this and other houses. Now that it is almost paid off, we can access the value of the house only by selling it (and sleeping outside in a Minnesota winter?) or by taking on a new mortgage and relinquishing at least part of our ownership to lenders again.

In barely an hour, my trip to the gas station and back home had revealed three parts of a growing economic crisis:

- We are gouged on prices for essential goods and services.
- Our wages are driven down by globalization.
- When we can no longer afford a decent lifestyle, those who have become wealthy at our expense lend us back our money so we can keep spending. We slide deeper and deeper into debt.

Not surprisingly, very few of us are benefiting from this scenario. A US Census Bureau report showed that the number of people living in poverty had risen to 37 million in 2004. The ranks of the working poor swelled and the annual earnings of full-time workers had fallen $1,000. Median household income was less than it had been in 1999. There were 700,000 more working people without health insurance than there had been a year earlier; the share of US workers with health insurance was the lowest since 1993.

In spite of these and many other gloomy figures, we are told not to worry, because the United

States is becoming what some politicians call an "ownership society." What we lack in wages we will make up for by smart investments in real estate and the stock market. Why worry about your falling wages when the value of your house is climbing higher than you ever imagined? Why worry about price gouging when you own part of the corporation that is setting those high prices?

Most Americans no doubt agree, at least in a general way, on what a successful economy must do. For example, it must provide a sound education for all its citizens. It must provide highways and other essential public services. It must provide police, fire, and military protection of life, property, and liberty. It must be one that is compatible with basic human rights and democratic principles. It must reward hard work and entrepreneurial innovation. It must be one in which everyone, be they children, wage earners, or retirees, can expect at least a modest standard of living and the health care to live life to the fullest.

But it's getting harder and harder for me to see how our current economic course will get us where we want to be. As I write this, the overall personal savings rate in the United States has fallen below zero. Wouldn't we be better off if people were able to measure their finances by what they had been able to save rather than by what they were able to borrow? Meanwhile, we have repeated calls to be more competitive in world markets. But note that those countries that excel at low-cost production tend to be very poor. Wouldn't we be better with a goal of having the highest standard of living in the world? The solution to more and more economic problems seems to be cutting taxes. Isn't the better goal to have an economy that provides enough to all of its citizens so they can afford the taxes necessary for education, public services, and an advanced society? We are rapidly developing into a society in which a very few people have a larger and larger share of the nation's wealth, something we haven't seen since the Great Crash of 1929. Wouldn't it be better if more people were comfortably middle class, even if it meant that fewer lived like royalty?

Will our society become more just and prosperous as we rely more on income from ownership and less on income from wages and salaries earned by working Americans? My own views on this question have been shaped by twenty-five years as a University specialist working directly with farmers on questions of profits, costs, policy, and markets. During many of those years, I also taught basic economics to hundreds of college students. From the farmers I learned the importance of profits, entrepreneurship, and hard work. From the students, I learned that traditional textbooks don't always match the reality today's young people face. My experience has led me to believe our current economic policies parading under the "ownership society" banner are leading us farther and farther from the economic society we would all like to see. Our current troubles in providing education, health care, decent jobs, and adequate savings are only a prelude of what is to come.

The United States has always been a successful economic model for the world. For this to remain true, however, we will have to pay greater attention to restoring and sustaining the middle class. Government must help with this task, but it cannot do it alone. Strong and effective unions are an essential part of any strategy that will restore and maintain the American middle class To see why, we must understand the economic forces of price gouging, wage cutting, and excessive debt that are weakening the middle class and leading us toward a landlord society that benefits none but the very few.

CHAPTER ONE

Centuries ago, we fought the Revolutionary War over taxation without representation. The same issue is back; only this time it is not England doing the taxing. Instead, it is corporations acting without government or unions strong enough to balance their market power.

Several years ago I asked each of the 105 students in my freshman economics class at the University of Minnesota to write a short paper on the hot topic of the day, the California energy crisis. Blackouts, "rolling brownouts" and skyrocketing prices for electricity were taking a serious toll on the economy of one of our largest states. Almost all of them wrote that the problem was caused by an imbalance of supply and demand. Some thought that the problem was one of not enough new power plants being available; others thought that the demand was simply too high and we needed more conservation.

One student came up to me after I made the assignment and said he thought the problem was that energy corporations were manipulating the markets. I told him that he was entitled to his opinion, but that we didn't study that in our class. We studied free market systems in which such activities were not possible, so he would need to choose another topic. A few years later, of course, it was clear to anyone studying the California crisis that the student was right. Enron, not the causes I had encouraged my students to write about, was the problem.

Now attention has turned to another energy problem, the price of gasoline. And there are still the same supply and demand papers for students to write. But this time around, the words "price gouging" come up often when we hear about supply and demand. Price gouging happens when there is not enough competition among suppliers of some essential product or service, in this case gasoline, to keep prices in line with costs of production. For years OPEC has been a textbook example of entire countries acting to limit competition among them so they can sell crude oil at higher prices. Many now think the major oil companies are doing the same thing.

In March of 2006, the Senate Judiciary Committee called in top executives from the country's largest oil companies to find out why gasoline prices had risen 60 percent in five years and topped $3.00 per gallon in many places during the months following Hurricane Katrina. At issue was whether mergers in the industry had gone too far and thereby reduced competition to dangerously low levels. On the face of it, the evidence was compelling. First, there were the profits—$100 billion by the top players in a single year. Then there was the matter of the 2,600 mergers in the oil and gas industry that the Government Accountability Office had tracked since 1991. Of these, the Exxon-Mobil nuptials of Number One and Number Two had given birth to an annual profit of $36 billion, the largest ever for a single corporation.

All of this raised some interesting questions from the Senators. If these mergers were reducing costs like they were supposed to, why were gas prices rising instead of falling? Since OPEC was charging refineries so much more for crude oil, how could those companies be posting record profits? Shouldn't we be rethinking the $14.5 billion in tax incentives for energy companies that had been built into our last energy law? In the end, however, protests from the CEO's of their need for financial strength, that the profits weren't all that big when properly considered, and that the industry remained highly competitive seemed to win the day. One after another, the Captains of Big Oil assured the Senators that record high gas prices were simply a matter of supply and demand.

Meanwhile, the Attorneys General of Illinois,

Iowa, Missouri, and Wisconsin weren't buying the supply and demand story for natural gas. Consumers in their states were being stuck with heating bills $250 above the preceding year, even though consumption had gone down, not up, by five percent. The report they commissioned, "The Role of Supply, Demand and Financial Commodity Markets in the Natural Gas Price Spiral" (March 2006) put it very clearly: "Demand has *not* been 'surging', 'soaring' or 'skyrocketing,' as is frequently reported in the press . . . Over the past three years, it has declined slightly." To make matters worse, the extra money being raked in by the energy companies was not being used to expand supply. Little wonder, then, that the report and the Attorneys General that commissioned it rejected "the usual prescription about biting the bullet until the supply-side comes around" and called for increased public oversight of energy markets.

Business Week, in its February 28, 2005, issue, carried a story on Pfizer, the world's largest pharmaceutical corporation. The story provides a good example of why Americans are becoming increasingly concerned by costs for health care, especially prescription drugs for which patents limit competition. Everyone knows that developing new pharmaceuticals is expensive; Pfizer spent $7.7 billion on research and development in 2004. Less well-known is that advertising and promoting pharmaceuticals is considerably more expensive.

While the company employs 15,000 scientists and support staff to develop drugs, it employs 38,000 sales representatives to market them. Pfizer spent $3 billion on advertising alone in 2003, making it the nation's fourth largest purchaser of ads. Only General Motors, Proctor and Gamble, and Time Warner spent more. The total cost to Pfizer for sales and administration was $16.9 billion, over twice as much as the $7.7 billion spent on research and development.

Thanks to Lipitor, Viagra and other "blockbuster" drugs, Pfizer made the Top 10 list of most profitable corporations in the United States. Its shareholders saw $11.3 billion added to their wealth, an increase of 596 percent over the previous year. Nevertheless, I probably was not the only one dismayed to see I had three choices for erectile dysfunction drugs, but no choice whatsoever in 2004 for a flu shot. Meanwhile, a book concerning the flu epidemic of 1918 made the bestseller list. As many as 100 million people died world-wide in that outbreak, most of whom were in the same age group as those unable to get a vaccination in 2004.

If we focus on another vitally important sector of our economy, food production, research evidence shows that all is not well there, either. A study at the University of Nebraska and the University of Connecticut (*Review of Industrial Organization*, 2002) investigated the effects of mergers

and acquisitions among 33 food industries rang-
ing from meatpacking to candy products. As
these industries continued to grow they could
become more efficient and therefore supply markets with products at lower prices, or they could
use their increased market power to increase prices
for their products. The results? Only 14 experienced lower costs because of increased concentration, and nine actually saw their costs increase as
they got bigger. Mergers and acquisitions actually
led to higher food prices in 24 of the industries
and lower food prices in only three of them.

As important as it is, ownership of products is
not the only ticket to such breathtaking profits.
A corporation can also own the market in which
goods and services are bought and sold. At first
blush, a privately owned market seems like an
odd idea. Markets are thought of as "free markets"
in economics texts. Granted "free" usually means
unencumbered by government interference. It also
implies, however, that no one imposes a cost for use
of markets. Producers meet consumers in markets,
be they street bazaars or internet sites, in ways that
do not involve costs over and above those required
to operate those markets.

Increasingly, the market in which many goods
and services are exchanged is owned by a small
collection of very large and very powerful corporations. The example most often cited is Wal-
Mart, the world's largest corporation. Wal-Mart

controls such a substantial share of the market for many retail products worldwide that it can "squeeze the supplier" and pass some of the savings along to consumers in a never-ending search for larger market share. Of course, not all of the gains are passed on to consumers. The owners keep enough to maintain their status as the country's richest family.

Health insurance companies provide another example of private markets that are by no means "free." Insurance companies do not produce drugs or examine feverish children. Nor do they seek medical care. They simply provide a costly mechanism for the exchange of goods and services between buyers and sellers. Consumers of health care services see insurance premiums as a costly "cover charge" for entering the health care market. An article in *Business Insurance* (4 April 2005) indicated that combined profits for the three largest health insurers were over $6 billion. The profit increases from the previous year for the three giants were 41.8%, 235%, and 60.0%. The "highlight of the year" was the "tremendous level of consolidation" which "improve[d] the companies' negotiating clout with providers."

As energy, health care, and food fall into the hands of fewer and larger corporations, private interests in effect gain the ability to assess taxes on all of us. What, after all, is an excessive increase in prices other than a sales tax? It has all the bad effects of a tax because it reduces the buying power of consumers. Worse yet, private taxation by price gouging has none of the positive effects that public taxes bring. For example, if gas taxes are charged by public agencies, they help build and maintain roads. But when oil companies charge taxes, they simply fatten up corporate profits and the bank accounts of the world's wealthiest people. Centuries ago, we fought the Revolutionary War over taxation without representation. The same issue is back; only this time it is not England doing the taxing. Instead, it is corporations acting without government or unions strong enough to balance their market power.

CHAPTER TWO

While price-gouging taxes us by over-charging for essential goods and services, wage cuts caused by globalization act as a private income tax by reducing our take home pay.

In spite of reassurances from our government that the economy is growing, the Census Bureau looked back at 2004 and saw a different picture: "real median income of both men and women who worked full time declined between 2003 and 2004 . . . the median income of men declined by 2.3 percent . . . the median income of women declined by 1.0 percent." The so-called growth in the economy benefited only those at the very top of the income ladder. Everyone else was left to live on lower wages and make do with reduced health and retirement benefits. Even a college degree lost its traditional power to increase middle class earnings; adjusted for inflation, earnings for those with a bachelor's degree fell for the fourth straight year.

The reason for this, as every working person knows, is globalization. Globalization is the evil twin of price gouging. While price-gouging taxes us by over-charging for essential goods and services, wage cuts caused by globalization act as a private income tax by reducing our take home pay. At the same time consumers are faced with higher prices, globalization demands wage and benefit concessions so we can be "more competitive" with low-wage countries. Not surprisingly, corporations and the think tanks they support consider globalization some sort of secular religion. But it is simply another way for the rich to get richer at everyone else's expense.

Suppose someone is making $20 per hour working in the United States for a global corporation. The corporation moves the job to a far less developed country, now pays $2 per hour, and then ships the product back to the United States where people have enough money to pay for it. What happened to the $18 per hour wage savings? Most obviously, it ended up as corporate profits. Increased corporate profits make the world's wealthiest people even richer, while the net loss in wage income makes the world's workers poorer. The income gap widens still further, with all the problems entailed. Furthermore, wage losses in the United States make it a poorer market for products of any kind, imported or not. This, in turn, threatens the jobs of even the $2 per hour worker because those jobs depend on more developed economies where people can afford to buy more than the bare necessities.

To better understand the long-term problems of global wage cutting, let us go back to eighteenth-century England and the world of Adam Smith. Smith laid the foundations for free market economics in *The Wealth of Nations,* a book that memorably describes a factory in which pins were made. Without the factory, Smith suspected that a person working alone could make no more than 20 pins in a day, perhaps as few as one. With the factory, workers were able to specialize in smaller tasks:

> One man draws out the wire, another straights it, a third cuts it, a fourth points it, a fifth grinds it at the top for receiving the head; to make the head requires two or three distinct operations; to put it on, is a peculiar business, to whiten the pins is another; it is even a trade by itself to put them into the paper. . . .

This specialization led to a remarkable increase in output per worker. Smith estimated that ten people so employed could make 48,000 pins per day.

This increase in worker productivity was central to Smith's optimism concerning the future of capitalist economies. He foresaw "a universal opulence which extends to the lowest ranks of the people." Why? Through the application of labor-enhancing technology each worker could make far more than was required for his or her own use. A worker previously making one pin a day could now make many thousands in the same amount of time. Consequently, "a general plenty diffuses itself through all the different ranks of society." All of this, of course, happens only if someone invests in new technology and puts it to use.

I confronted a version of the pin factory many years ago when I began advising farmers on economic matters. An ornamental nursery is one in which landscaping plants are grown. Plants are typically grown in relatively small pots and transplanted to increasingly larger ones as time goes on. The process of repotting thousands of plants can be labor intensive. The nurseryman I advised had several employees doing this repotting with almost no specialization of labor. Each employee would go to a designated area to repot plants and work at that task whenever he or she had time. At a local trade show, a repotting machine caught the nurseryman's attention. The machine was simple, not unlike Adam Smith's pin factory. It consisted of a table with various mechanical devices that allowed a crew of six to ten to specialize in removing plants from pots, mixing potting soil ingredients, putting plants into pots, and the like. Workers were more productive with the machine; in fact, we thought the labor cost per pot could be cut in half.

In spite of these advantages, adoption of the machine was not guaranteed. It made sense only if there were sufficient labor cost savings to pay for the machine. In Adam Smith's world, those labor savings came exclusively from reducing the number of labor hours required to perform a task. The same was true when I first looked at the potting machine problem: making workers more productive could reduce labor costs, but the wages paid those workers could not be reduced. Imagine the nurseryman as a global corporation powerful enough to influence wages. With lower labor costs the machine would cost the same, but the dollar value of the labor savings with the machine would be less. The nursery would therefore be less likely to invest in the potting machine.

Generally, we likely would expect labor saving technology to be adopted when wages are higher than when they are lower. More is saved with mechanization when wages are high. After World War II, the United States and Western Europe experienced an economy with powerful unions, closed borders, and other factors that kept wages high. Consequently, there were equally powerful incentives for businesses to develop and adopt labor saving technologies. In so doing, those businesses further increased labor productivity in the usual sense: they made it possible for more to be done with a given number of workers. More productive workers made more money, wages went up all the more, and incentives to adopt labor saving technology remained strong.

In the world of corporate accounting, labor productivity is not measured in physical terms such as more product for a given number of workers. Rather, it is measured solely in dollar terms, that is, fewer dollars spent on labor for a given level of output. Paying workers less for the same job has the same positive impact on corporate profits as does making workers more productive in the classic sense. There are some obvious advantages, at least in the short run, for businesses to pursue the reduced wage road to increased productivity. The risks of research, development, and adoption of expensive labor saving equipment are avoided. One can leave technology as it is and increase profits by letting workers do what they are already doing, just for lower wages. Globalization makes this possible by weakening the social contracts that keep wages high. Unions are less effective in a global context, labor moves more easily across borders, and products can be made in low-wage countries and sold in high-income countries without the annoyances of tariffs or other trade restrictions.

What difference does it make? Corporate profits, or the share of production going to those who own productive assets, should be the same with fewer workers making more, or more workers making less. That much is true, but we must return to the central importance of the pin factory. The pin factory was the key to the "universal opulence which extends to the lowest ranks of the people." Without it, the benefits of capitalism as we usually know it are reduced because the very incentives to develop and employ capital are diminished in times of lower wages.

Exuberant accounts in the business press about higher corporate profits resulting from increased labor productivity must be read carefully. If labor productivity is gained through lower wages, what is really being touted is the growing economic power of global corporations. The exercise of ownership power will, in the longer run, become a burden on the overall performance of the capitalist economy. It may reduce consumer purchasing power; it may retard innovation; or it may do both. But in no case is it cause for celebration.

CHAPTER THREE

The very rich are not investing as much as they could. Instead, they make their profits by lending money to the rest of us to make up for our lost purchasing power. In 2004 alone, new home equity loans of nearly $650 billion amounted to 6.9% of after-tax income. This, of course, can only go on for so long, and then something has to give.

Price gouging and wage cutting does nothing to help the middle class. Instead, it dumps truckloads of extra cash into the bank accounts of the country's wealthiest people. What do they do with their newfound savings? The hyper-rich might invest it in new factories and technology. Then, again, they might not. Price gouging and wage cutting work just fine without new investments of this type. Instead, the very wealthy lend out money. Borrowing replaces savings for those caught in the bind of paying more and making less. This, in turn, leads to massive indebtedness on the part of the middle class, an increasingly unstable financial system for everyone, and ever more money going to the wealthy as interest payments.

It is no secret that the citizens of the United States, as a whole, have not been saving much in recent years. The percentage of disposable income devoted to savings fell from 7.7 percent in 1992 to 1.4 percent in 2003. By 2005 the savings rate had fallen below zero. These are average rates of savings for everyone in the United States economy, rich and poor alike. We might reasonably suspect that the story would change if we could see data for different income groups. A study done for the National Bureau of Economic Research[1] allows us to do that. The study used several data sets to compare savings rates among people in five different ranges (called "quintiles") of income. After examining a data set called the "Consumer Expenditure Survey," the authors found that "among households with heads between 40 and 49, median saving rates range from –23 percent in the lowest income quintile to 46 percent in the highest." Results for another data set, the Survey of Consumer Finances, observed: "[W]e see the

1. Dynan, K.E. and J. Skinner and S.P. Zeldes. "Do the Rich Save More?" NBER Working Paper No. 7906. Cambridge, MA. September 2000.

estimated median saving rate rising significantly from –2 percent for households in the bottom quintile to 27 percent for households in the top quintile. Savings rates are even larger for the richest households: 37 percent for those in the top five percent of the income distribution and 49 percent for those in the top one percent."

The national savings rate, while low, is therefore a composite of a great many people with very different rates of savings. While one might quibble with the exact numbers presented, the overall conclusion of the study seems consistent with common sense: "The rich, indeed, save more." People in the top one percent of those sampled saved almost half of their income. Even this amount is probably low for the hyper-wealthy. Unfortunately, information on people with incomes exceeding $500,000 per year was not included. On the other hand, people at the opposite end of the income scale saved nothing and depended on borrowed money to maintain their lifestyles.

Even as the hurricane disasters on the Gulf Coast exposed widespread poverty, the business press was full of stories on a global savings glut. For example, the eighty technology corporations included in the Standard & Poor's 500 stock index were reported to be holding $229 billion in cash and equivalents in 2005 (*Business Week,* 18 July 2005). In 1999, the same companies had less than half that amount. Granted, operating cash is a good thing, up to a point. But these corporations are way beyond that level. Seeing no useful investment purpose for their newfound riches, the corporations have few options. Sometimes, mergers and acquisitions make the economy less competitive. But most of the time, the money earns no more in corporate bank accounts than the very wealthy could get on their own. The excess cash is therefore passed out as giant dividends. Microsoft, for example, paid out over $35 billion to owners in 2004 and still managed to keep $38 billion on hand for a rainy day.

The same story is playing out on a much larger global scale. In its cover story "Too Much Money," *Business Week* (11 July 2005) reported that the global savings rate is at its highest in two decades: "Surprisingly, even in the profligate U. S., businesses have been accumulating huge sums as undistributed corporate profits—running at a record annual rate of $542 billion in the first quarter—have almost doubled in the past two years." In other words, the very wealthy who own corporations have no productive use for profits. Even China, a country still building new factories, faces the prospect of substantial excess capacity. The advantage of cheap money to invest is largely offset by the declining fortunes of consumers who must see the article's title of "Too Much Money" as some sort of cruel joke.

On a global scale, the excess of income over consumption was $11 trillion in 2005. In other words, there was no productive use for an amount of money equivalent to the size of the entire U. S. economy. For example, the run-up in oil prices is pouring money into oil-rich countries at unprecedented rates. Owners there are choosing to recycle money into glutted financial markets rather than risk exploration and productive investment. Most of their money, along with China's $70 billion surplus and apparently everyone else's windfall gains, is going into the same place: the United States economy. Far and away the world's largest debtor, the United States stands alone in trying to parlay oceans of cheap cash into a consumer nation strong enough to support the world's economy. The push for profitable places to stash this bonanza has led to skyrocketing house prices on one hand and an economy saturated with ever-riskier financial deals on the other. It is little wonder that the *Business Week* article ended on the ominous note: "Hold on to your hats."

As new tax cuts on dividends came into play, dividend payouts were over 25% higher in 2004 than they were in 2000. Why invest in productive ways when the new tax code says, "Take the money and run"? These dividends and tax cuts put even more money into the pockets of the world's wealthiest people, who in turn funneled it into financial instruments such as low-interest mortgages that fuel speculation in real estate. The *Wall Street Journal* (16 June 2005) reported that even though business lending has been on the downswing, mortgage lending grew at an 11% annual rate since 2000. As the real estate market heats up, the same houses sell over and over for higher and higher prices, further enriching financial corporations, but increasing the debt load that must be serviced by the middle class. This, too, reduces our ability to purchase other things the economy might produce. The purchasing power of the middle class, upon which growth depends, is therefore hollowed out by a lethal combination of lower wages, non-competitive prices, and superheated real estate markets.

When entrepreneurs invest savings in new productive capital, the economy grows and prospers. This does not always happen, however. Since the days of John Maynard Keynes and the revolution he sparked in economic thinking during the 1930's, we have seen that savings can have a dark side. We are seeing that dark side now. The very rich are not investing as much as they could. Instead, they make their profits by lending money to make up for the lost purchasing power of middle class Americans. In 2004 alone, new home equity loans of nearly $650 billion amounted to 6.9% of after-tax income. This, of course, can only go on for so long, and then something has to give. We are falling into a variation on what Keynes called a "liquidity trap." The last time that happened on a grand scale will be remembered forever as the Great Depression.

CHAPTER FOUR

We cannot wait for things to straighten themselves out, for the downward spiral is self-perpetuating.

One of the comforting concepts in free market economics is that of equilibrium. Sooner or later, a free market economy will adjust itself and settle out in a way that makes the most efficient use of whatever resources are available. Unfortunately, such a happy outcome is not likely to happen today. Instead, we are in a downward spiral that, left unchecked, will stay on its course toward disaster.

We live in a world in which some countries are relatively wealthy, some are relatively poor, and many global corporations have at least some ability to operate as they see fit in both wealthy and poor countries. Corporations have an obvious incentive to sell their wares in the wealthy countries. In fact, many of the poorer countries provide virtually no market whatsoever for anything other than basic necessities. Where to produce the products, however, is a more difficult decision. Historically, most corporations were bound by tradition, by national laws, and by trade restrictions to produce in their "home" countries. As a result, relatively high wages were a principal source of the home country's wealth. National production appeared to create its own markets.

As tradition, national laws, and trade barriers slowly fall victim to globalization, corporations receive a new option. They can produce in the poorest countries and sell in the wealthiest. Cost cutting, combined with stable and wealthy markets, appears to be a sure path to increased income. Those who are first to move production to poor countries will weaken the markets in wealthy countries by reducing the number of high paying jobs in those countries. Most other corporations will remain national, however, and continue to contribute to their host country's wealth. The first corporations to globalize therefore see markets that are only slightly weakened combined with production costs that are dramatically lowered. For the time being, their profits increase. As more and more corporations follow suit, however, weakened markets will become more of a problem. At this point corporations must seek out lower wage production, not to increase their profits, but simply to survive in the new world order. Those who do not globalize are crushed ultimately by the impossible combination of high production costs and poor markets. Even if a corporation wants to remain national, it cannot do so if most others are global.

The outcome sees fewer, larger corporations selling to weakened markets and producing more of their products in poorer countries. All the remaining corporations now realize the advantages, or at least the necessity, of cutting labor costs. They continue to seek ever-poorer countries in which to make their products. These corporations, because of their growing size and wealth, have more political influence and encourage more countries to open their doors. They are also better able to force down wages for those remaining workers in wealthy nations. The threat of their jobs being moved to other countries is ever-present. Labor unions, once a principal mechanism for creating wealth among nations rather than among corporations, become shadows of their former selves, presiding over orderly wage concessions rather than aggressive moves for higher wages. A new round of cost cutting begins, and once again the first to find more ways to lower their wage costs are rewarded with new profits. Other corporations by necessity either follow suit or are added to the growing list of corporate mergers, acquisitions, and bankruptcies.

As corporations become larger and fewer in number, competition among them is reduced. This

adds price gouging to the already damaging effects wage cuts are having on the pocketbooks of
consumers. Profits, in turn, get even larger. There
is no incentive to reinvest these profits, however,
for they were gained at the expense of diminish-
ing markets. Those profits, instead, are used to
soften the wage losses in wealthy countries with
massive lending to consumers in wealthy nations.
What workers once purchased with money from
paychecks is now purchased with money borrowed from the very corporations that reduced
their wages in the first place. People unfortunate
enough to rely on productive work rather than
ownership to make a living now have an additional strain on their family finances—along with
falling wages and price gouging, they have higher
interest payments to make that further diminish
their ability to purchase new goods and services.

Corporations waking up later to the global-
ized world must work all the more to cut labor
costs if they are to survive, much less profit. Not
only current wages, but also pension plans and
other benefits previously promised workers come
to be seen as impediments to "competitiveness."
Parts of the globe better suited to providing cheap
labor must be found. New opportunities for price
gouging must be exploited. Similarly, latecomers
to this process will find only riskier places to lend
their profits. Consumers are drawn into financial

schemes in ways that once would have been seen as dangerously imprudent.

Such a process cannot go on forever. Sooner or later, the borrowing power of workers in wealthy markets is exhausted. The endgame is hardly appealing. The wealth once held by consumers and workers in wealthy countries will have been transferred to the owners of the few surviving global corporations. Those corporations will be without markets for anything but the most basic essentials, because workers will be working at wages common in the least, not the most, developed countries. Substantial creation of new wealth through capitalist methods will now be impossible. The world economy will be in a state of collapse brought on by powerful corporations, owned by a relatively few super-rich individuals. The middle class will have disappeared.

We cannot wait for things to straighten themselves out, for the downward spiral is self-perpetuating. As we shall see, however, not all is lost—we have the means to put things back on track if only we will use them.

CHAPTER FIVE

In 1921, the advent of the Jazz Age, the song "Ain't We Got Fun" memorably foretold the coming Depression: "The rich get rich and the poor get poorer." Farmers were already in a Great Depression of their own when the song came out, and the rest of the working people in the United States were nearer than they might have thought to joining them. There has been only one time since in which the rich got richer and the poor got poorer to such a dramatic degree. We live in that time today.

The same process that is grinding away the middle class is making a handful of people rich beyond belief. Profits from Microsoft have put William Gates at the top of the list of richest people in the United States for several years running. The Walton family is even wealthier. Upon his death, the wealth of Sam Walton, founder of Wal-Mart, was divided among his four children. When *Forbes* magazine published its list of the 400 wealthiest Americans in 2004, these four families were estimated to have a combined net worth of a mindboggling $90 billion.

What does someone do with so much money? Imagine a very nice house costing $10 million. Ninety billion would buy 9,000 such houses. Or, a fleet of 360,000 princely cars costing $250,000 each could be at your beck and call for Sunday afternoon drives with the family. Setting aside a billion or so for the kids to go to college should cover unforeseen tuition hikes. Another billion for one's golden years surely would keep the wolf from the door. A $15 billion shopping spree in early 2005 would have bought all the shares of General Motors stock.

The combined wealth of the Forbes 400 in 2004 came to something in the neighborhood of $1 trillion. By comparison, the combined wealth of all United States citizens was $45 trillion, meaning that 400 people owned over two percent of the combined wealth of nearly 300 million people. These 400 people could go slumming for a year and buy everything world-wide sold by Wal-Mart and still leave three-quarters of their wealth intact. The gross national income of China had not reached $1 trillion in 1999. In February of 2004, President Bush submitted a budget for the United

States of $2.4 trillion, including a projected deficit of $521 billion.

How did these people get so rich? First let's put to rest the rags to riches story of people just like us working especially hard and getting wealthy on the remarkable wages they were able to earn. Although it has worked for some, even garden-variety millionaires, the hyper-wealthy don't fall into this category. To see why, let's rework the previous examples. Given a salary of $250,000 per year, it would take 360,000 years to earn $90 billion. If somehow one could negotiate a raise to $10 million per year, the task could be accomplished in just 9,000 years. But the Walton fortune, for example, was built in less than 50 years. These are the fruits of ownership, not hard work.

Any basic economics text will tell you this: a good corporation acts to maximize the wealth of its owners. Cold blooded as it sounds, this rubric has enjoyed solid legal support dating back to 1919 and the *Dodge v. Ford Motor Company* decision handed down by the Michigan Supreme Court. Henry Ford proposed that his automobile company be operated in such a way as to pay relatively high wages to its employees so more of them could afford to buy Ford cars. But members of the Dodge family were substantial shareholders and challenged the proposed policy in court. Why give workers money that could otherwise enrich shareholders? The Court ruled in favor of the Dodge family and said, "A business corporation is organized and carried on primarily for the profit of the stockholders." And, indeed, the richest people in the United States own the vast majority of all outstanding stocks. As a practical matter, therefore, we could revise *Dodge v. Ford Motor Company* and say: "Corporations should be operated in such a way as to make the wealthiest people in the United States even richer."

We might also rephrase the corporate purpose slightly to say that the purpose of a corporation is actually to *increase* the income gap between the rich and poor. It should come as no surprise that very wealthy individuals own most, but not all, corporate stock. Some is in the retirement funds of common people. Suppose, for the purposes of argument, a few wealthy people hold 90 percent of the stock in a particular corporation and the remaining ten percent is dispersed among those hoping to live well in retirement. If that corporation pays out $10 million during a certain year, the wealthy few will immediately be richer by $9 million. The rest of the shareholders will split the remaining $1 million. It's simply a matter of mathematics—percentage changes reward those with the biggest base more than those with a smaller starting point.

The twin goals of increasing the gap between rich and poor along with making the rich even richer have been met with remarkable success. In 1921, the advent of the Jazz Age, the song "Ain't We Got Fun" memorably foretold the coming Depression: "The rich get rich and the poor get poorer." Farmers were already in a Great Depression of their own when the song came out, and the rest of the working people in the United States were nearer than they might have thought to joining them. There has been only one time since in which the rich got richer and the poor got poorer to such a dramatic degree. We live in that time today.

The economic well-being of a country's citizens can be measured by their average income, ebbing in lean times and flowing in the good. Average income is the measure we most often have in mind when we say, for example, that the citizens of the United States are better off economically than those of Rwanda. Another measure is called "income distribution." This indicator does not simply take the total income available and divide it by the number of citizens sharing that income. Instead, income distribution measures who has the lion's share of that income. If available income is distributed fairly evenly among its citizens, that economy supports a strong middle class. If the economy has virtually no middle class, the rich will have most of the money while the poor share very little.

Income distribution in the United States has

been the subject of much commentary in recent years. By any measure, the gap between rich and poor is steadily widening. For example, the Economic Policy Institute found that between 1979 and 2000 the real income of poorer households grew by 6.4%. Meanwhile, the income of the richest families grew by 184%. Furthermore, studies have shown that not all of the most developed countries have similar income distributions. Some spread growth in income and wealth more evenly among their citizens. On this score, the United States has one of the poorest track records.

Thomas Piketty and Emmanuel Saez (*The Quarterly Journal of Economics,* February 2003) used individual income tax data to carefully construct a consistent series of data for the United States during the period 1913 to 1998. Their work showed that "Ain't We Got Fun" was right on target. Beginning around the time the song was written, the income share of the top ten percent began a dramatic rise. The rich were getting richer, and the poor were getting poorer. The situation persisted throughout the Depression years of the 1930's. (Remember this does not mean that average income was high in the Depression. Rather, it means that the distribution of available income was especially favorable to the wealthy in that period.) With the advent of World War II and the end of the Great Depression, the income share of the top ten percent quickly declined, and we entered a period in which the United States economy was solidly middle class in nature. But in the late 1970's the share of income going to the top ten percent once again began to rise. By 1998, the last year for which this study had data, the income distribution favored the wealthy just as it had in the beginning of the Jazz Age.

Two other equally important economic measures, wages and profits, also reflect the "rich get richer" trend in our economy. Both indicators have an eerily "Roaring Twenties" look about them. Wages and corporate profits also provide the clearest distinction between those who *do something* for a living and those who *own something* for a living. Someone earning a wage or salary is compensated for productive activity that contributes to the growth of an economy. A person collecting dividends, on the other hand, is taking advantage of their ownership status to collect part of the proceeds from economic activity.

Corporate profits have been especially bountiful in recent years, but wages have struggled to keep up with inflation. The same thing happened during the Jazz Age. Measured by Gross National Product, the Roaring Twenties were aptly named. However, the average worker making $1,342 per year in 1920 had wages that were virtually the same at $1,384 in 1928. Then came the Crash. By 1933, both Gross National Product and wages, adjusted for the massive unemployment of the

times, were half of what they had been a few
years earlier.

People should be able to live well; in fact, I
wish more of us did. But not at the scale of the
hyper-wealthy. Once people have more money
than they can possibly spend on goods and services, they no longer use it in ways that stimulate
the economy. Instead, they use the power their
money brings to manipulate the government and
the economy in order to make themselves even
richer. They get more tax breaks, less regulation,
more support for globalization, and policies that
favor lenders over borrowers. The middle class
continues to weaken.

CHAPTER SIX

In 2004, the United States government collected a total of $1.1 trillion from individuals and corporations. In that same year, corporations charged the public $1.2 trillion more than was necessary to pay all of their operating expenses. That's correct—corporate profits were higher than the total collections of all federal taxes.

In September of 2005, President Bush was reported as saying, "Working people have had to pay a tax, in essence, by higher gasoline prices" (*StarTribune,* 17 September 2005). He surely got that one right. In today's economy, we pay taxes to both government and private corporations. Unfortunately, there is no IRS equivalent to report tax collections by corporations powerful enough to manipulate prices and wages. The best we can do is to infer what might be going on from the financial performance of corporations. Here the news is shocking. In 2004, the United States government collected a total of $1.1 trillion from individuals and corporations. In that same year, corporations charged the public $1.2 trillion more than was necessary to pay all of their operating expenses. That's correct—corporate profits were higher than the total collections of all federal taxes.

Every dollar drained away by private taxation is one dollar less the public has available to pay taxes imposed by the government. Because of this, resistance builds to government taxes that provide the public investments in education, transportation, health care, and other services so necessary to maintaining a high quality of life. But cutting public taxes can only go so far towards keeping money in the pockets of consumers. The money saved in public taxes might be taken immediately by higher private taxes. Reduced public taxes, for example, might be seen as a way to free up the consumer dollars necessary to pay even higher prices for gasoline and prescription drugs. Likewise, services that were once provided by the public now come back as expenses individual consumers must pay.

A good example of this privatization of once-public expenses is higher education. Overall, personal consumption expenditures were 15.1 percent higher in 2003 than in 2000. Some expenditures grew more rapidly, however. Not surprisingly, those items included housing at 18 percent and medical care at 27.8 percent. But the cost for higher education was rising even faster at 29.9 percent. In my own work as a college professor I have seen double-digit tuition increases play havoc with the finances of both students and parents in each of the years since 2000. And, sadly, the increases were not the result of higher education suddenly becoming more expensive because quality was skyrocketing. Rather, the increases were the direct result of university administrators scrambling to fill the void left when public monetary support became scarce.

Taxing income is another, even clearer, example of how taxes reduce personal income. If I don't see a certain portion of my check because it is deducted for federal and state taxes, I obviously don't have it to spend. The government does this all the time. When private corporations tax income, they don't do it with payroll deductions of the common variety. Rather, they work to dismantle unions and promote trade regulations that have the overall effect of lowering wages. The difference between what workers would have made with and without these self-serving policies is also an income-reducing tax. For example, Department of Commerce data show that manufacturing wages in 2003 were, in total, off by 12 percent from what they had been in 2000.

The incessant drumbeat for lower state and federal taxes is understandable but misguided. Lower public taxes will not lead to a stronger economy as long as private taxes go unregulated. While state and federal taxes are important to maintaining a vibrant society, private taxes have the opposite effect. Worse yet, any program that lowers state and federal taxes frees up more money that can be siphoned off by price gouging and wage cutting. We certainly need a dramatic new national tax policy that will substantially lower the taxes we all pay. But that policy should be aimed not at the public sector, but at the private sector. We must be prepared to heavily tax excessive wealth that builds up in spite of our efforts to prevent it, for only then will money stay in the hands of consumers that can keep it circulating in ways that lead to economic growth. We must also do more, much more, to directly address the causes of private taxation: corporate concentration and globalization.

President Bush was right when he said we were being taxed by rising gasoline prices. But he was wrong when he said we would have to pay for Hurricane Katrina with borrowed money and cuts in public services. That we are already in debt up to our eyeballs as a nation is clear to everyone. And no one who watched publicly-maintained levees giving way, underfunded emergency services struggling to provide water and sanitation to dying citizens, and thousands of people too poor to evacuate suffering unimaginably in a major U. S. city could have been thinking we would benefit from still further cuts in public services. Instead, we should focus squarely on redistributing the wealth built up by private taxes the middle class had already paid.

CHAPTER SEVEN

The middle class cannot buy its way into prosperity with corporate stock and real estate any more than it can by buying lottery tickets. This strategy of buying stock or real estate is popular among its proponents not because it is effective, but because it plays by ownership rules. Those rules favor the very wealthy over middle class and poor alike.

If ownership is seen as the train to prosperity, it is only natural for everyone to try to get a good seat. For example, "You seem to doing well with the stocks you own, so I'll buy some, too." Or, "Your house has gone up in value; maybe it's time for me to buy one." Such strategies, by their very nature, cannot work. The middle class cannot buy its way into prosperity with corporate stock and real estate any more than it can by buying lottery tickets. This strategy of buying stock or real estate is popular among its proponents not because it is effective, but because it plays by ownership rules. Those rules favor the very wealthy over middle class and poor alike.

Programs to make home ownership more widely available to low-income households, for example, are in vogue these days. Sometimes these programs provide money for down payments. Other times, they provide public insurance for mortgages that otherwise don't qualify for traditional funding. In any event, the assumption is that once low-income families establish a beachhead on the shores of the ownership society, their economic prospects will be brighter. Unfortunately, that doesn't always happen.

When the relatively poor attempt to enter the ownership society by buying a home, one of the first and most substantial obstacles they face is that so-called "sub prime" loans carry higher interest rates. Furthermore, the current federal tax code allows the deduction of mortgage interest. This deduction, however, has value in direct proportion to household income. A relatively wealthy person might take out a six percent mortgage and claim all interest paid as tax deductible. A poor borrower may pay nine percent but, because they use the standard deduction, see no tax savings whatsoever from their home purchase. The same can be said of property taxes. Those in a position to itemize can deduct those taxes while those using a standard deduction cannot. Because of such factors, the poor pay more to own homes than do those with higher incomes who purchase similar properties. Thus the financial benefits of ownership are smaller for the poor than for those of greater means.

The poor also take substantially higher risks in entering the ownership society. For example, a special program may allow a poor family to purchase a home with no money down. Immediately, the mortgage payments are higher because of the amount financed (in addition to the factors outlined in the previous paragraph). Any downturn in the housing market will mean that the house is worth less than the mortgage. The poor are more likely to lose employment and more likely to experience a health care financial crisis because they are less likely to be insured. This means that poorer homeowners also are more likely to need some cushion in their mortgage, but they are less likely to have it. As a result, they are at risk to undergo foreclosure and lose everything that has been paid for the privilege of belonging to the ownership society. As this is being written, nine times as many sub prime loans are in foreclosure as are prime loans of the type available to higher income families.

A third reason the home ownership solution does not work well for the poor is that they more often need extra money for emergencies. Any equity that has been gained in the home is

often subject to additional borrowing in the form
of home equity loans. Homeownership for these
people is not a way to accumulate wealth. Instead,
it is a way to accumulate more debt than would
otherwise be possible. This increased debt puts
the household at still further risk of foreclosure
and the loss of all funds devoted to owning a
home.

None of this is to say that the poor should not
own homes. Rich or poor, most everyone agrees
that home ownership encourages better care of
the nation's housing stock and leads to more effective engagement in community affairs. But
that's only a cover story for an ownership society.
For proponents of an ownership society, owning
a home takes on the additional benefit of being
a cure for poverty. Here policy falls short. There
are financial benefits for encouraging the poor to
own homes, but those benefits are more likely to
accrue to the wealthy, those that already belong
to the ownership society. Obviously, if I am in a
position to make sub-prime loans to the poor, I
can collect substantial fees at the time of sale, fol-
lowed by relatively high interest income. I also can
look forward to getting the house back in a foreclosure so I can repeat the process. All the while, I
might enjoy the protection of a federal loan guarantee on the mortgage as well. It is odd that the
lender, rather than the low-income homeowner,
would have such protection if the goal really were

to increase the wealth of the poor. Loan guarantees do not protect the poor who cannot make payments on a loan. They are foreclosed anyway. The guarantee compensates the lender for any lost payments.

Even if home ownership programs for the poor can easily backfire, don't they have the opposite effect among the middle class? After all, the value of a middle class family's home is almost always their principal financial asset, and the value of that asset often increased at double-digit annual rates in the late 1990's and the early part of the twenty-first century. An immediate problem, of course, arises when home values increase at rates substantially above general inflation and growth in wage rates: fewer people find housing affordable and, for all practical purposes, more people are low-income in relation to what it would take to purchase a home. The number of people who fall into this situation grows along with housing prices. More people have too much of their income devoted to mortgage interest payments and more people are at risk of foreclosure. In times of need, more people are tempted with home equity loans that give back any gains in equity to lending institutions.

Consider the situation of a family holding a $220,000 mortgage on a home valued at $250,000. While the family certainly considers itself to be the homeowner, the lender has an 88 percent

interest in the property while the family has only
12 percent. Were the property sold with normal
sales commissions and fees, it would return almost nothing to the family. A visitor from another planet might ask whether the term "owner"
should apply to the family at all. At best, they are
potential owners in that they have the opportu-
nity to repay $220,000 and then take clear title to
the property. But until that happens, the lender
seems to hold as least as a good a claim to the title
"owner."

If the family in the example is fortunate, over
time their house will go up in value. If they cash
in by selling the house, however, the family loses
its place of residence and must spend any gains in
securing another place to live. The lender, on the
other hand, receives a substantial portion of the
family's income every month in the form of mortgage payments. Especially in the early years of a
loan, those payments are comprised chiefly of
interest and contribute very little toward building equity on the part of the homeowner. Furthermore, the lender can sell the mortgage at any
time without giving up his or her place of residence. If more rewarding places to spend money
present themselves, the lender is under no obligation to put money back into housing. Finally, the
lender is relieved of any obligation to maintain
the property or to pay property taxes, for those
are universally the obligation of the family. The

family is even required to pay for insurance on the full value of the home, therefore insuring the lender's share as well as their own.

Ownership as presented in these examples primarily benefits those who are already wealthy, those with sufficient means to be on the receiving end of mortgage payments. Those who make housing payments in an effort to join the ranks of the wealthy are fundamentally handicapped in the process. Homeownership is a great thing in many ways, but we can't conclude that the ownership society has any benefits for most of us. A house is a great place to live but a poor source of income for whomever lives in it.

Now let us turn to the strategy of "investing" in corporate ownership instead of home ownership as way of jumping onto the ownership bandwagon. The supply of new stock shares is relatively stable; corporations grow mostly by mergers and acquisitions. The overall economy that fuels corporate profits, and therefore dividends, also grows relatively slowly, maybe in the range of three to five percent per year. So how can the Dow soar to such heights?

Dividends certainly play a role in determining stock values, but so does anticipated growth. The sum of the two components gives the total return. As an example, if a stock costing $200 paid an annual dividend of $10, that part of the stock's returns would be five percent per year. If the expected growth in the value of the stock were three percent per year, then the total return would be eight percent. Now imagine that massive retirement funds are directed into the stock market so that more can participate in the ownership society. Eight percent return, after all, isn't all that bad. Every share purchase requires a share seller, however, so the new buyers must bid up stock prices in order to buy them. This adds to the growth portion of returns. Yet that growth has nothing to do with productive economic activity. It is simply a function of how much people have to pay for admission into the ownership society. The portion of returns accounted for by real economic activity falls and the portion fueled by speculation increases.

The plight of those lured into stock market purchases by retirement plans and Social Security privatization (or "personalization," to use the parlor term) is especially distressing. They receive none of the annual dividend payments in cash. Instead, those payments are "reinvested" into the financial maelstrom. It is as if the dollars one received from a chain letter were automatically sent to others on the list. Instead of providing current income, the dividends fuel the fire of speculation. Writing for the *New York Times* (4 February 2005), economist Paul Krugman reported on the results of a computer analysis of Social Security privatization he had performed with a colleague at the Center for Economic and Policy Research. Stock market returns averaging 6.5 percent per year above inflation would require economic growth way above what anyone was forecasting. Using more reasonable growth rates, his research showed that price-earnings ratios would have to be 70 in 2050 and over 100 in 2060 for the stock market to continue at a 6.5 percent pace over the long haul. Many are wary of today's ratios of 20 or so.

Statements of what one is worth seldom make much distinction between stock market holdings and money in the bank. Money in the bank is very different, however. One doesn't need to sell it for purchases. But stock market wealth must be sold if the growth gains are to be achieved. Unfortunately, the very process that built the wealth is making it more and more unlikely that buyers will be available when it is time to sell. Future participants in this pyramid scheme are suffering from the price gouging and wage cutting that create corporate profits to begin with. Working people therefore pay for their piece of the stock market pie twice—once when they work for low wages to bake it and again when they pay high prices to buy it.

Clearly, those who sell while the pyramid is still standing will be better off than had they put their money under some financial mattress. There is another type of winner, however, who stands to gain much more. Those winners are the very wealthy owners of stocks. Since they don't need to buy stock at current rates, they benefit from the fictitious growth in value. More importantly, they don't need to reinvest dividends to acquire more stock in the process of building a retirement nest egg. They take those dividends as cash and get richer in the sense most of us think of as being rich—they have more cash on hand. Less fortunate players use their dividends to buy stocks and drive up the value of the holdings of the fortunate few. Viewed this way, the stock market is an ideal mechanism for tilting the income distribution more and more toward the wealthy. Wealthy owners are rewarded every quarter with dividend payments; average Joes and Janes who take money away from current consumption and cast it into the stock market are rewarded with nice-looking, but possibly meaningless, statements of growing net worth. The only thing that can be said for sure of this latter group is that they have less cash on hand. Money they could have saved in conventional ways is now blowing in the Wall Street wind.

Suppose a person has the exclusive legal right to run a lottery. Each week, he or she sells tickets for $1 to anyone who wants to get rich. At the end of the week, a single winner is awarded half of the collected money. Who's going to come out ahead in the long run, the person who has very little money but wants to get rich by buying tickets, or the person who owns the lottery? Week in and week out, the lottery owner will take half of the money "invested" by the players. Even though one of the players will do very well each week, the players as a group lose money week in and week out. The lottery turns out to be an ideal way for the rich get richer and the poor to get poorer. The same goes for the more respectable stock market and real estate lotteries that drive our financial system closer to the edge with each passing day.

CHAPTER EIGHT

The ideas being used to justify free trade and deregulation of business, among other things, measure their age in centuries. The world of commerce has changed so much that these ideas, while as brilliant as ever, no longer match the conditions for which they were developed. We must therefore be especially cautious when those who act in ways that are "inimical to the public interest" misuse economic principles to justify their behavior.

It's quite the trick to convince people that they will somehow be better off if their well-paying job in the United States is traded for cheaper toasters at Wal-Mart. Convincing those same people that it's in their best interest to pay breath-taking prices for prescription drugs isn't any easier. Phrases like "being competitive," "free trade," and "supply and demand" are a big part of this unlikely sales job. They hide the fact that traditional economic theory is being used as a system of smoke and mirrors and not as the powerful analytical tool it was meant to be. Reference to an idea that was developed centuries ago is applied to a situation that could not have been imagined when the theory was being formulated. We're told global corporations are simply larger versions of mom-and-pop enterprises that compete with each other on a level playing field. Even traditional economics texts find this hard to swallow, but still the ideology persists.

Free trade theory is a good example. It is usually justified with a tradition going back to David Ricardo in early nineteenth-century England. The so-called "corn laws" made importing grain into England very difficult. This, in turn, made food more expensive. Ricardo, in his famous theory of "comparative advantage," showed how trade between two nations could benefit both under certain circumstances. If one country was more efficient at producing one thing, and a second country was more efficient at producing another, it made sense for both to specialize in what they did best. Each would have a surplus to trade with the other, and the total of both products available to share would be higher than that available if each pursued a goal of national self-sufficiency.

The early examples of Ricardo's theory, and many from today's texts as well, concern agricultural products. For example, tea doesn't grow well in the United States. On the other hand, the midwestern United States is remarkably well suited to the production of grains. It makes sense for the United States to trade some of its grain for tea produced in another country. A classroom lecture on the subject would go on to calculate how much tea and grain would be traded and what the benefits would be. An important point in the lesson is that those calculations are done in pounds of tea and bushels of grain, *not* in dollars. Comparative advantage theory is about trading physical products in ways that move us toward more efficient production. Specialization is the key to gaining that efficiency.

Compare this to a modern rendition of free trade: a corporation moves its appliance factory from the United States to a low wage country, then ships the appliances back to the United States where they are subsequently sold. The corporation sheds high-paying jobs in the United States in favor of low-paying jobs wherever the factory now resides. The difference is pocketed by the corporation and recorded as an increase in labor productivity. Notice that there is no gain in efficiency in the appliance example. Just because someone is willing to work for less does not make him or her more efficient at what they do. Remember that Ricardo's theory was spun from bales of cotton and bushels of wheat, not from dollars and Euros. The only way the example could lead to more efficiency in the sense Ricardo used the term is if workers in the low-wage country were somehow physically better suited to producing appliances than their counterparts in the United States. To make such a claim smacks of racism. In fact, there is no reason to believe that a highly trained worker in the United States is less efficient than a worker new to the industry in a low wage country. But that's not the point among present day free trade enthusiasts. Even if workers in the low wage country are only half as efficient, a corporation still could profit by hiring twice as many at the prevailing low wages. This would make the world economy less efficient, not more so.

Efficiency suffers further with free trade because the incentive wanes to adapt technology that increases labor productivity. We have already seen in the nursery-potting example how low wages reduce the need for new technology. Here's a larger scale example from *Business Week* (July 4, 2005) concerning Renault's newest vehicle, the "ultra-cheap, no-frills Logan": "The simple design means assembly at the Romanian plant is done almost entirely without robots. That lets Renault capitalize on the country's low labor costs. Gross pay for a Dacia line worker is $324 per month, vs. an average $4,723 a month for auto workers in Western Europe."

Moreover, free trade has nothing to do with

Mr. Ricardo's theory because today's free trade is not at all about trade in the sense that Mr. Ricardo envisioned. What is "traded" in the appliance example? The same corporation makes the same appliances and sells them to the same people no matter where it chooses to locate the new factory. All that changes is how much the corporation must pay its workers. The corporation shrewdly says that the appliances are products of the low wage country and appeals to Ricardo's distaste for tariffs that serve as protectionist barriers to trade. The fact that there was never any trade to protect gets overlooked. The trade barrier instead protected the overall well being of the national economy, a goal that Mr. Ricardo no doubt would have applauded.

If the study of economics has a Bible, it is the text I have used with hundreds of college students. Nobel-laureate Paul Samuelson has been brilliantly introducing the fundamentals of free market economies to "Econ 101" students for over 50 years. He now authors the text with Yale economist William Nordhaus. Like each of its predecessors, the 18th Edition begins with a half-semester or so of what is known as supply and demand theory. Terms such as "utility," "marginal product," and "average revenue" may bring back memories to veterans of a course in microeconomic principles. Just before spring break, students are shown the importance of what they have learned, "the essence of the invisible hand—the remarkable efficiency properties of competitive markets."

Ironically, the first thing they read upon returning to their studies is this:

> Perfect competition is an idealized market of atomistic firms who are price-takers. In fact, while they are easily analyzed, such firms are hard to find. When you buy your car from Ford or Toyota, your hamburgers from McDonald's or Wendy's, or your computer from Dell or Apple, you are dealing with firms large enough to affect the market price. Indeed, most markets in the economy are dominated by a handful of large firms, often only two or three. Welcome to the world you live in, the world of imperfect competition.[2]

This description is good fit for the real-world modern food system. Studies routinely show that the top four or five corporations in all types of food handling and processing have combined market shares of at least 40 percent and sometimes exceed 80 percent. Five corporations control half of all supermarket grocery sales in the United States.

---

2. Samuelson, P.A. and W.D. Nordhaus. *Microeconomics,* 18th Edition, McGraw-Hill Irwin. 2001, p. 166. Used with permission.

The "idealized market of atomistic firms who are price-takers" is a long way from reality, a very long way. In fact, the description of imperfect competition suits industries across the board, not just food. This is not to be taken lightly, for the text later says, "such industries behave in certain ways that are inimical to the public interest." Let me once again remind you that these quotes, including this one, are not from a radical pamphlet handed out on street corners. They are from a well-respected college textbook.

I truly enjoy economics and have immense respect for Adam Smith, David Ricardo, and the other remarkable thinkers who developed the theory of competitive markets. At the same time, I can agree with Donald L. Kohn, Governor of the Federal Reserve, when he told a group of bankers in 2005 that "Our economy is in unexplored territory in many respects." The fact of the matter is that the ideas being used to justify free trade and deregulation of business, among other things, measure their age in centuries. The world of commerce has changed so much that these ideas, while as brilliant as ever, no longer match the conditions for which they were developed. We must therefore be especially cautious when those who act in ways that are "inimical to the public interest" misuse economic principles to justify their behavior.

Economic theory, for most people, is intimidating. I've seen it with my students, I've seen it with the farmers I work with, and I suspect it is true for most people who are reading this book. But no matter what economic theory might be thrown your way by corporate spin doctors, you probably think deep down that nothing good will come of wage cutting, price gouging, and whole-sale substitution of borrowing for savings. For what it's worth, at least one economist—namely, me—agrees with you completely.

CHAPTER NINE

An ownership society is a landlord society. It is one in which money that could be used to reward labor, management, and productive investment gets skimmed off by the fortunate few.

Those who own massive blocks of corporate stock are usually referred to as investors. In farming, there is a better word for those who make money because of what they own instead of what they do. They are called landlords. Farmers do the real investing in machinery, seeds, and the like that drives the rural economy. Landlords, like corporate shareholders, simply sit back and take part of what others have earned. Corporate profits are determined in a way that is complex in practice, but perfectly understandable at the conceptual level. The corporation deducts all of its expenses from its sales and calls the remainder its profits. Those expenses include materials, buildings and machinery, labor, management, and interest on all money borrowed to establish and operate the corporation. In other words, all expenses needed to run a corporation are paid before any profits are declared and distributed. The amount left for shareholders to claim is therefore that money which was left over after the corporation already had enough money to operate fully and cover all of its expenses.

An ownership society is a landlord society. It is one in which money that could be used to reward labor, management, and productive investment gets skimmed off by the fortunate few. The ideology of ownership would have us believe that this is just how things work in our economic system, so the less we tamper with the way profits are distributed among owners, managers, and workers, the better off we all will be. In reality, the wealth of owners is determined as much by politics as by economics. Economics plays the game, but politics sets and enforces the rules.

Many times I've asked myself why a farmer's labor and management is so lightly valued in comparison to land. On a crop with a gross income of, for example, $400 per acre, it's not unusual to see the combined returns to labor and management somewhere in the range of $25 per acre. On the other hand, the landlord could well be collecting $125 per acre or more in the country's midwestern breadbasket. When the farmer doesn't own the land, the return to land goes to someone who may never see the land at all during the year. In many cases, the landlord lives far away and serves only to collect a rent check from the farmer. Aren't there other ways to divide the income from farming? Why should the country's farmland be valued, in total, at figures approaching $1 trillion some years while the country's farmers routinely clamor for government payments to supplement their income? The answer is simple: political decisions made long ago set up and enforce the rules that led to this distribution of farm income. A different set of rules could have us looking at a new economic picture that favored farmers over landlords.

The "extra" farm income, that is, the money landlords are able to claim without affecting the overall level of farm production, comes from natural resources and public projects. The income farm landlords receive is clearly related to the productivity of farmland. Better tracts of land bring higher rents than do poorer ones. There is more to the story, however. To reach its full potential, farmland must be served by a transportation system capable of getting crops to market in a timely and efficient manner. Those who farm the land must be well educated and have access to productive technology. The economic system in which farming occurs must be fair and stable. All of these latter benefits, and many more, come at public expense. Public dollars build and maintain transportation, provide public education at all levels, and have been very generous in supporting research into advanced farming methods. Public funds have provided farm programs that have stabilized the farm economy in many ways.

The same can be said of the profits corporations receive. Sometimes, they are the direct result of the nation's natural resource base. Those resources may be used for productive purposes, such as drilling for oil or cutting timber. At other times, the natural resource base itself contributes in that it is polluted by economic activities that would have been much more expensive to conduct had the resource base been properly protected. Air and water quality degradation are prime examples of ways corporate activity does not pay its full share, and therefore profits more than it otherwise would. The same public expenditures for roads, schools, a stable government, and research build the infrastructure that corporations use at a fraction of the full cost. This, too, leads to excessive profits.

Because of its generous share of natural resources and centuries of public action to build social infrastructure, the United States is a wealthy nation. During the twentieth century, there were two principal methods for making sure this wealth was distributed in ways that it would do the most to maintain and build the nation's wealth. First, the very wealthy were heavily taxed either directly or through the corporations they largely owned. This provided for maintenance of existing social investments and creation of new ones. Our system of public education and research, for example, was well supported by tax dollars. Second, labor unions became strong enough to shift corporate profits from very wealthy owners to the middle class in the form of better wages and benefits. This allowed money to stay in the hands of those most likely to spend it in ways that would further stimulate the national economy.

In a few short decades, globalization has raised the specter of moving all of this wealth into the hands of a very few. In so doing, it will destroy the very process that created and maintained our wealth in the first place. Corporations are now strong enough to call for, and get, substantial tax reductions. They can call for, and get, substantial wage concessions. They can call for, and get, weakened public oversight of their activities. These changes that have permitted and fostered the growth of corporations and globalization are political, not economic in origin. They result from the exercise of power. Changing things for the better will therefore not be a search for new economic ideas. It will instead be a process of changing the balance of power in ways that favor those of us who are not corporate landlords.

CHAPTER TEN

Working people in the United States are quite capable of understanding their economic problems. That's not the problem. The problem is that they don't have the economic power necessary to develop their ideas and carry them out.

We must rebuild our economy on policies other than globalization and tax cuts for the very rich. Who will lead us? In the past, we have looked to government. Today, however, there are compelling reasons to think that government may not have the will, or even the ability in some cases, to do what is needed on their own. Unions will have to play a much stronger role in our economy if the middle class is to survive and prosper.

Some of the private ownership taxes each of us pays are recycled back into massive political contributions. These contributions further weaken the resolve of politicians to work on behalf of the middle class. To make matters worse, there comes a point at which the ability of government to act on behalf of anyone but the very wealthy becomes endangered. This happens as corporate size grows beyond that which nations were conceived to govern. A good friend said it best: "If an elephant sits down in your living room, it doesn't matter if it's a good elephant or a bad elephant; it is still going to break something."

In April of 2004, *Forbes* published a listing of the world's largest corporations. The combined sales reported for the 50 largest corporations on the list were $3.8 trillion. Corporate revenues are sometimes compared to gross domestic product figures for individual countries. The combined revenues of these 50 corporations are better compared to the GDP of the world, which was $36.5 trillion in 2003. Only the GDP's of the US ($10.9 trillion) and of Japan ($4.3 trillion) were larger than the combined revenues of these 50. The top ten corporations alone had revenues almost as large as the GDP of China. Profits, let alone revenues, for the 50 largest corporations on the list were larger than the GDP's of 130 of the world's countries, including Argentina, Norway, Saudi Arabia, and South Africa.

World's Largest Corporations		
	Revenues	Profits
Top 10	$1.3 trillion	$112 billion
Top 20	$2.4 trillion	$212 billion
Top 50	$3.8 trillion	$315 billion

Source: *Forbes* (12 April 2004)

A hundred years ago trust busting national programs held robber barons at bay. The corporations of those days were certainly large, and certainly powerful, but they weren't global. Moving a railroad system to Thailand was not a convincing threat at the end of the nineteenth century. A clear implication of globalization is a reduction in the degree to which any one nation can control the actions of a company operating across national boundaries. Countries compete with each other for the lion's share of entire industries, just like small towns and states have fought over manufacturing plants for decades. Instead of competing for individual retail stores, countries vie to become "competitive" global markets.

The trend, to say the least, is not encouraging. We're quickly trading government regulation of corporations for corporate regulation of government. NAFTA, CAFTA, and the WTO are prime examples. At the same time, the principal activity of government seems to be that of compensating

those who lose when corporations choose paths
that aren't in a nation's best interest. Farm legisla-
tion that pledges billions of dollars to deal with
the fallout of low farm product prices is a good
example. On other fronts, we see pleas to provide
public subsidies to those who cannot pay high
prescription drug prices and welfare for those
who lose their jobs to globalization.

Clearly, the more we can do to support public
officials who side with the middle class in effective ways, the better off we will all be. But we
must do more. In the same way we act together
in political parties to advance our political interests, we should act in the market place to advance
our common economic interests. Labor and consumer unions have done just this during much
of the twentieth century. In fact, those years in
the mid-twentieth century when the income distribution most favored the middle class were also
the years in which unions were strongest. This
is no coincidence—strong unions are essential in
both building and maintaining the middle class.

One of the principal reasons unions are more
important than ever is that ownership philosophy encourages each person to act as an individual and make his or her own fortune. This appeal
to individual initiative can play right into the
hands of the country's corporate landlords—when
it comes to economics, not all people are created
equal. Some are vastly wealthier than others, and

because of this, they are vastly more powerful. They can take the gains that less powerful individuals work so hard to get, and there is nothing the less powerful individuals can do about it. The secret to economic power is the ability to play one person against another. Either large corporations will play one individual against another, or those individuals will form unions strong enough to play one corporation against another.

My work with farmers is now almost exclusively focused on finding ways that farmers can work together to sell what they grow in volumes much too large for any one farm to produce. This matches the selling power of the farmers with the buying power of processors and retailers. Organizing farmers into effective economic units is a long and difficult struggle, but it is the only way I see to fully address the problem of too much economic power in too few hands. The government's ability to continue expensive farm programs is threatened by tax cuts; the government's ability to continue those programs is also being challenged in the World Trade Organization by globalization philosophy.

Labor unions are adjusting to some of the same challenges facing farmers. Nonetheless, we must not lose sight of the ways that collective economic action can dramatically improve the performance of our economy:

- First, most of us probably agree that there
  must be sufficient public taxes to build and
  maintain a wealthy economy. Such taxes
  are possible if wages are high enough so
  people can pay the taxes necessary for high
  quality public services. Effective unions
  can make sure wages are not driven to
  levels where we can no longer afford the
  society we all want.
- Second, we will be more secure if we act
  together to pursue our collective economic
  interests. For example, instead of holding
  out privatizing social security as a ticket
  to the ownership society, the higher wages
  unions bring about will allow most of us to
  realistically save for retirement in conventional, secure ways.
- Third, by acting together in the market
  place to keep wages high and prices under
  control, we assure that wealth stays con-
  centrated in the middle class. High wages
  and reasonable pricing directly convert
  what would be high corporate profits in a
  rich-get-richer economy into an economy
  where more money reaches the hands of
  people who will use it to stimulate economic growth.
- Fourth, unions can focus enough votes and
  money to begin the daunting political task
  of undoing much of the damage that has

resulted from misguided trade policies and unenforced anti-trust laws.

These are, of course, general guidelines for what must be done. A more specific solution has taken me a long time, both as an academic and as a person working closely with farmers, to understand. Working people in the United States are quite capable of understanding their economic problems. That's not the problem. The problem is that they don't have the economic power necessary to develop their ideas and carry them out.

With due respect to my academic colleagues and the theories they have developed, there is nothing complicated about the ideas driving our economy. "Let's find a way to pay our workers less and keep more for ourselves" is a strategy any high school student could easily dream up. The same goes for "Let's charge more for what we produce and pocket the difference." These simple ideas are guiding much of modern business not because they are new or complicated. We are playing by these rules because the people who benefit from them are powerful enough to enforce them. "Let's have decent wages so we can take care of ourselves and our country" and "Let's pay prices high enough to make sure products are produced, but no higher" are also simple ideas. The problem is that those who believe in them are not powerful enough to make them stick.

There's another problem with the "great idea" solution, too. Economies don't just change, then stay that way. They are ever-changing systems that demand this policy one day, and another policy on the next. It's like driving. You can figure out in advance where you want to go and how you generally want to get there. What you can't do in advance, however, is anticipate what you will do as every unanticipated bump in the road comes along. Only powerful players can make the year-to-year decisions necessary to keep the economy on track. If power is in the wrong hands, the economy will drive farther and farther into the ditch. If power is in the right hands, however, we can make the decisions necessary to stay comfortably on the main road no matter what comes along.

Rebalancing power in the economy is essential if the middle class is to thrive. Doing this, however, will require more than our government alone can deliver. We must act together in the market place as well.

CONCLUSION

Time is not on our side. The sooner we take action to put economic power back where it belongs, in the hands of the middle class, the better off we all will be.

Our overheated, rich-get-richer economy is nothing to worry about in the ideology of ownership. We are encouraged to charge ahead in spite of the reddest of red flags. Friends old enough to remember the Great Depression are not so cavalier. Nor am I, because I've seen firsthand what has happened to farming and rural communities in the United States.

In spite of farm program payments as high as $20 billion in some years, the story of low farm income is persistent. Consistently fewer farmers work increasingly larger tracts of rented land, use rented seeds, raise livestock they don't own, and are being forced to compete in global markets they can't control. The rural communities in which these farmers live and work suffer equally. As farming declines while its income drains away to distant owners, country towns lose population, then hospitals, then schools, then more population, and finally disappear altogether. The farm crisis of decades past is often rechristened as a crisis in rural America.

In the mid-1990's, a University of Minnesota rural sociologist studied the income distribution (that is, the degree to which income is in the hands of the very poor, the very rich, and those in between) for the state of Minnesota. He found that wealthy suburban counties in the state had income distributions common in highly developed Northern European countries. But the rural counties displayed income distributions more typical of a developing country such as Sri Lanka.

Decades ago, thriving family farms and prosperous rural communities stood waiting to be dismantled by the forces of absentee ownership, first of land, then of farm markets and supplies, and soon of the food system as a whole. This is but a preview of what those same forces of ownership, left unchecked, can and will do in the general economy. We are traveling down a road that leads first to economic stagnation, then to another massive depression. The middle class gets smaller and more threatened with each passing day.

Time is not on our side. The sooner we take action to put economic power back where it belongs, in the hands of the middle class, the better off we all will be.

To order additional copies of *Middle Class ★ Union Made*

Web: www.itascabooks.com

Phone: 1-800-901-3480

Fax: Copy and fill out the form below with credit card information. Fax to 952-920-0541.

Mail: Copy and fill out the form below. Mail with check or credit card information to:

Itasca Books Distribution
3501 Highway 100 South, Ste 220
Minneapolis, MN 55416

Order Form

Copies	Title / Author	Price	Totals
	Middle Class ★ Union Made / **Richard A. Levins**	$19.95	$

Subtotal	$	
7% sales tax (MN only)	$	
Shipping and handling, first copy	$	4.00
Shipping and handling, ___ add'l copies @$1.00 ea.	$	
TOTAL TO REMIT	$	

Payment Information:

__ Check Enclosed __ Visa/MasterCard		
Card number:	Expiration date:	
Name on card:		
Billing address:		
City:	State:	Zip:
Signature:	Date:	

Shipping Information:

__ Same as billing address __ Other (enter below)		
Name:		
Address:		
City:	State:	Zip:

To order additional copies of *Middle Class ★ Union Made*

Web: www.itascabooks.com

Phone: 1-800-901-3480

Fax: Copy and fill out the form below with credit card information. Fax to 952-920-0541.

Mail: Copy and fill out the form below. Mail with check or credit card information to:

          Itasca Books Distribution
          3501 Highway 100 South, Ste 220
          Minneapolis, MN 55416

Order Form

Copies	Title / Author	Price	Totals
	Middle Class ★ Union Made / **Richard A. Levins**	$19.95	$

Subtotal	$
7% sales tax (MN only)	$
Shipping and handling, first copy	$ 4.00
Shipping and handling, ___ add'l copies @$1.00 ea.	$
TOTAL TO REMIT	$

Payment Information:

__ Check Enclosed   __ Visa/MasterCard

Card number: Expiration date:

Name on card:

Billing address:

City:	State:	Zip:
Signature:		Date:

Shipping Information:

__ Same as billing address   __ Other (enter below)

Name:

Address:

City:	State:	Zip: